Goosebumps

Scaredy-Caps Special

Goosebumps available now:

Look out for:

Goosebumps

Scaredy-Caps Special

R.L. Stine

Scholastic Children's Books,
Commonwealth House, 1 – 19 New Oxford Street,
London WC1A 1NU, UK
a division of Scholastic Ltd
London ~ New York ~ Toronto ~ Sydney ~ Auckland

First published in the USA by Scholastic Inc., 1995
First published in the UK by Scholastic Ltd, 1996

ISBN 0 590 13704 2

Printed by Cox & Wyman Ltd, Reading, Berks.

10 9 8 7 6 5 4 3 2 1

COLLECTOR'S SLAMMER

Curly—number one *Goosebumps* fan!

Hi there! Curly here, number one *Goosebumps* fan, welcoming you to the *Goosebumps Scaredy-Caps Special*. It's got sixteen of the coolest caps around.

But first check out the slammer. That's me. And make no bones about it. I'm the coolest slammer around! You can use me in the super *Goosebumps* cap slappin' game you'll find on page 43 of this totally awesome book.

Totally awesome. Because it's got information that *Goosebumps* fans have to know—and can't find anywhere else.

First you'll read THE STORY behind each *Goosebumps* scaredy-cap. Keep going. Because THE STORY BEHIND THE STORY comes next—and you won't want to miss that—or any of the FRIGHTENING FACTS, TOP SECRETS! FOR GOOSEBUMPS FANS ONLY!, TOTALLY AWESOME moments, or jokes we've thrown in to HAVE A GOOD SHRIEK at! The pages are filled with inside information about your favourite

1

Goosebumps books and secrets about R.L. Stine you never knew.

Then move on to our PETRIFYING PUZZLES AND GRUESOME GAMES—if you have the *guts* to do them. I don't!

Have a totally excellent time with your *Goosebumps Scaredy-Caps Special*. And have a scary day!

THE MASKED MUTANT
from
ATTACK OF THE MUTANT

GOOSEBUMPS 23
Published October 1995

THE STORY

Skipper Matthews collects comics. His favourite one is about The Masked Mutant, an evil supervillain who wants to rule the universe. Then one day Skipper loses his way in a strange part of town, where he and his new friend, Libby, discover The Mutant's secret headquarters! Does The Masked Mutant really live in Riverview Falls?

THE STORY BEHIND THE STORY

Skipper really loves comics, but do you think he'd give up the hair on his head to read them? R.L. Stine did.

When R.L. was a kid, he loved to read spooky comics called *Tales from the Crypt* and *Vault of Horror*. Unfortunately, his mother did not let him buy them or read them in their house. The only place R.L. could read his favourite comics was at the hairdresser, where they always had the latest issues. So R.L. got a haircut every week!

TOP SECRET! FOR GOOSEBUMPS FANS ONLY!

In *Attack of the Mutant*, The Masked Mutant's foes are called The League of Good Guys. There are six superheroes in the league. Skipper mentions only three of them: The Amazing Tornado-man, The Galloping Gazelle and SpongeLife (The Sponge of Steel). The other three members are: Rott Weiler— The Human Guard Dog, Clara the Claw Woman (she has fifteen-centimetre nails) and The Fantastic Ferret (the underground superhero).

TOTALLY AWESOME! The parts of the book you'll never forget

Remember when Skipper thought Libby had melted The Masked Mutant—but she hadn't? You don't remember? To find out who she did melt, go around the circle clockwise, writing down every other letter. You'll get the answer!

START HERE ↓

N N T T H M E O M L A E G C N U L E F E I M C A E

Answer on page 54.

THE LIVING MUMMY
from
THE CURSE OF THE MUMMY'S TOMB

GOOSEBUMPS 4

Published January 1994

THE STORY

Exploring an ancient pyramid in Egypt with Uncle Ben will be totally awesome! That's what Gabe thinks when he visits his uncle and his cousin Sari. Then Gabe finds himself deep inside the pyramid. Alone. And trapped! Gabe says he doesn't believe in the curse of the mummy's tomb. Maybe now he'll change his mind!

THE STORY BEHIND THE STORY

Remember all the disgusting facts that Gabe tells Sari about mummies? Who could forget the one about the ancient Egyptians using a tool to pull the dead person's brain out through his nose! All the facts are true. And Gabe knows a lot more creepy stuff about mummies. Here are some frightening facts he wants you to know:

● Sometimes, in ancient Egypt, if a mummy was too tall for its coffin, someone would break its legs to make it fit!

● Before a body was mummified, all the internal organs—like the stomach, liver and lungs—were removed, except for the heart. Ancient Egyptians left the heart in the body because they believed it was the centre of all feelings.

● A hundred years ago, everyone was wild about mummies. So wild, in fact, that they held mummy unwrapping parties. And they used real mummies!

HAVE A GOOD SHRIEK!

Gabe's uncle Ben loves to tell mummy jokes. Here's one he told Gabe and Sari. You'll have to use the code over the page to unravel the answer to this one!

Why didn't the mummy have any hobbies?

Answer: ★✠ ✿✿● ✿✳✳ ✳✦✠✿ ✖◆

✦✿ ★✦● ✿☆✳▲

CODE

A = ✡   D = ♣   E = ✠

H = ★   I = ♧   K = ▲

L = ✳   N = ❀   O = ☆

P = ◆   R = ✳   S = ●

T = ✳   U = ✖   W = ✺

Answer on page 54.

EVAN ROSS
from
MONSTER BLOOD III

GOOSEBUMPS 27

Coming in April 1996

THE STORY

Evan can't stand babysitting for his genius cousin, Kermit. Kermit is always playing practical jokes on Evan and his friend Andy. But now they have the perfect way to even up the score with Kermit— Monster Blood! But the joke's on Evan when things go more than a little wrong. And Evan starts growing bigger ... and bigger ... and bigger...!

THE STORY BEHIND THE STORY

Goosebumps fans have been wondering just how big Monster Blood can make things grow. Now you can work it out!

In *Monster Blood III*, Evan starts as five feet tall, and after eating only a little bit of Monster Blood, he grows to twenty feet tall. That's four times larger. So if you fed the same amount of Monster Blood to a ten-feet-tall elephant, it would grow to approximately forty feet tall!

FRIGHTENING FACTS

It may be a coincidence, but *Monster Blood III* has a cast of characters with real superstar names. Check it out—there's Conan the Barbarian, Trigger (Roy Rogers' horse) and Kermit (unfortunately, he's no frog!).

CARLY BETH'S MASK
from
THE HAUNTED MASK
GOOSEBUMPS 11

Published September 1994

THE STORY

Carly Beth has the scariest Halloween mask around. In fact, it's the ugliest, most terrifying mask any kid has ever seen. The day goes by, and Halloween slowly comes to an end for everyone. Everyone except Carly Beth. That's when she discovers how terrifying her mask really is! It won't come off!

THE STORY BEHIND THE STORY

One Halloween night, R.L. Stine's son, Matt, slipped on a creepy Halloween mask. When Matt tugged at the mask to take it off, it wouldn't budge. When R.L. saw this, he jumped right on the

11

case—he ran to the computer and started writing *The Haunted Mask*! (Oh, if you were wondering, Matt did eventually manage to pull the mask off—by himself!)

TOP SECRET! FOR *GOOSEBUMPS* FANS ONLY!

Every *Goosebumps* fan knows the story of Carly Beth's mask, but here's a story you've never heard.

Once, long before Carly Beth moved into her neighbourhood, a handsome teenager lived on Carly Beth's street. He was a good student, but he was failing chemistry. His chemistry teacher was very mean. He refused to spend any extra time helping the boy.

The boy took matters into his own hands. He crept into the chemistry lab late at night to practise a few experiments of his own. That's when it happened. He accidentally mixed the wrong chemicals in his test tube. The tube exploded all over him. But instead of burning his face, the chemicals aged him. He became an old man overnight! An old man with a thin moustache and a pinched face. He was desperate to get his old—or, rather, his young—face back. So he started experimenting with making masks—masks that came alive! You guessed it. He's the shopkeeper in *The Haunted Mask*. And the one who created the mask that Carly Beth bought!

THE MUD MONSTERS
from
YOU CAN'T SCARE ME!

GOOSEBUMPS 15

Published February 1995

THE STORY

Nothing scares Courtney. Nothing. Now that would be okay—if Courtney weren't such a big show-off. But she likes making Eddie and his friends look like frightened wimps. Well, Eddie's had enough. It's time to scare Courtney—no matter what. So Eddie convinces Courtney to come out to Muddy Creek. Where the Mud Monsters live. Who believes in Mud Monsters? Only Courtney does. But maybe Eddie should, too!

THE STORY BEHIND THE STORY

According to the Muddy Creek legend, the Mud

Monsters come out of their muddy graves once a year to seek their revenge on the townspeople. But there are rumours that the Mud Monsters were spotted one other time.

A few years after the Mud Monsters sank into their muddy graves, a land developer decided to dig up Muddy Creek. He wanted to turn it into a water park. But as soon as the digging began, horrible accidents erupted at the work site. The workers and their machinery were sucked into the mud—never to be seen again. Only one worker survived. He told a terrifying tale. He said the workers were pulled under the mud by the Mud Monsters. And there, they became Mud Monsters themselves. Of course, no one believed him. Do you?

TOP SECRET! FOR *GOOSEBUMPS* FANS ONLY!

Nothing scares Courtney. But what *Goosebumps* fans want to know is: does anything scare R.L. Stine? Secret sources say that R.L. is not afraid of the dark, or insects, or snakes, or heights, or monsters. But there is one fear he can't conquer. He's afraid of deep water! With his spooky imagination, R.L. always thinks about the creepy things that could be lurking under the water. Things you can't see ... until they GRAB you!

TOTALLY AWESOME! The parts of the book you'll never forget

Remember the spooky words Eddie's teacher, Mr Melvin, told the class about monsters? Unscramble the sentence, and you'll see them!

dream real scary The we as as up
can isn't the monsters world.

Answer on page 54.

THE HAUNTED SCARECROW
from
THE SCARECROW WALKS AT MIDNIGHT

GOOSEBUMPS 22

Published September 1995

THE STORY

Jodie and her brother Mark are visiting their grandparents' farm. But this summer, everything on the farm seems different. Only Stanley, the farm hand, is the same—he's as weird as ever. But Grandma and Grandpa are quieter than usual. Much quieter. And their single scarecrow out in the cornfield has gone. In its place loom twelve evil-looking ones. And at midnight ... they come alive!

THE STORY BEHIND THE STORY

The Scarecrow Walks at Midnight was inspired by a true experience. Once R.L. Stine walked near a cornfield and saw a scarecrow move! At the time he thought the wind was blowing it. But now he's not so sure…

FRIGHTENING FACTS

Stanley brings the scarecrow to life with his book of ancient superstitions. Want to take a peek at some other creepy superstitions listed in Stanley's book? Check these out:
- If a child likes hitting people, after the child is dead and buried his or her hand will stick up out of the ground—and dogs will use it like a lamp-post!
- If a fly falls into your drink, it means good luck.
- Eating a roasted mouse will cure whooping cough.

TOTALLY AWESOME! The parts of the book you'll never forget

According to Jodie, her brother Mark's vocabulary consists of only three words. And after reading *The Scarecrow Walks at Midnight*, you probably agree! Can you remember the three words? If you can't, we've given them to you over the page. But you'll have to unscramble them!

SRGOS; EDRIW; OLOC

Answer on page 54.

THE HUMAN BEE-ING
from
WHY I'M AFRAID OF BEES

GOOSEBUMPS 17

Published April 1995

THE STORY

Everybody makes fun of Gary Lutz. Everybody. Gary doesn't have a single friend—but he does have a dream. More than anything in the world, Gary wants to be somebody else. Well, Gary's dream is about to come true. Gary is about to get a new body. But not the one he had in mind—because this body has six legs and wings and stings!

THE STORY BEHIND THE STORY

Remember what a brat Gary's little sister, Krissy, was in *Why I'm Afraid of Bees*? Well, the rumour is that when Gary went to make his body-switching plans, he tried to set up a match for Krissy. Unfortunately, after running her profile through the computer several times, the people at Person-to-Person Vacations came to the conclusion that nobody wanted to be Krissy—not even for a week! True? Could be.

FRIGHTENING FACTS

Did you notice all the insects that bug Gary? You didn't? Well, Gary wasn't the only insect mentioned in the book. Besides the hundreds and hundreds of bees that have room and board at Mr Andretti's, there's…

● Gary's favourite video game, EcoScare 95. It's all about fighting poisonous ants.

● A dragonfly that tries to kill off Gary the bee.

● Person-to-Person Vacations. It's located on Roach Street!

TOP SECRET! FOR *GOOSEBUMPS* FANS ONLY!

Gary's a pretty allergic kid. Do you know what happens to him whenever he eats honey? To find out, cross out the letters in the word BUZZ!

ZZUHBEUB
GBZUEUZTSB
BHBIZUZVEBBSZ

Answer on page 54.

IT'S GREEN, IT'S LEAFY, IT'S DAD!
from
STAY OUT OF THE BASEMENT

GOOSEBUMPS 3

Published November 1993

THE STORY

Margaret and Casey Brewer are really worried about their dad, Dr Brewer. He's a scientist. And he's experimenting with some new kind of plant in the basement. What's the big deal about growing plants? Nothing, really. Until Margaret and Casey spy little green leaves sprouting from their dad's head!

THE STORY BEHIND THE STORY

Stay Out of the Basement was inspired by an old TV show where kids grew strange plants in their basement. In that story, though, the plants were mushrooms—mushrooms from outer space that wanted to rule the world! And you thought Margaret had it tough!

HAVE A GOOD SHRIEK!

If Dr Brewer doesn't stop sprouting leaves on his head, what will Margaret and Casey do? To find out, unscramble the letters below

EAKM EIKL A ERET DAN EVALE!

Answer on page 54.

MR MORTMAN—THE MONSTER IN THE LIBRARY!
from
THE GIRL WHO CRIED MONSTER

GOOSEBUMPS 8

Published June 1994

THE STORY

Lucy Dark loves to tell monster stories. She makes them up, of course. She has an incredible imagination. One day, Lucy discovers a real live monster—the summer school librarian. But no one will believe her. And that's too bad. Because this monster has a frightful plan. A plan to get Lucy!

THE STORY BEHIND THE STORY

R.L. Stine named this book after an Aesop's fable called *The Boy Who Cried Wolf*. In that story, a shepherd boy thought it would be fun to run into town yelling that a wolf was attacking the town's flock of sheep. The villagers were very angry when they hurried to help him and saw no wolf. Well, one day a wolf did attack, and the shepherd yelled (or cried) "Wolf!" again. But no one believed him. No one ran to help him. And the wolf had all the lamb chops he could eat!

Because Lucy Dark always told monster stories, no one believed her, either, when she cried "Monster!" for real.

TOP SECRET! FOR *GOOSEBUMPS* FANS ONLY!

As you know from reading *The Girl Who Cried Monster*, the Darks are not your average family. They look normal and they do normal things, but they have a big secret. Which leads to a big question: where do the Darks come from?

The Dark family is originally from Romania. They were forced to leave their native land because the country was swarming with monsters. So they sailed to America. They settled in Timberland Falls because they heard it was definitely monster-free. And the neighbours weren't nosy. It was just what the Darks needed. A safe place to bring up kids. And a safe place to keep their big secret—until the summer librarian came to town!

TOTALLY AWESOME! The parts of the book you'll never forget

Most *Goosebumps* have a surprise ending, but *Goosebumps* fans will agree that the dinner scene at the end of *The Girl Who Cried Monster* is one of the best and biggest shockers of all! Some fans say the ending of *Attack of the Mutant* is a bigger surprise. What do you think?

WOLF—MAN'S BEST FRIEND
from
THE WEREWOLF OF FEVER SWAMP

GOOSEBUMPS 14

Published January 1995

THE STORY

Something creepy lives in Fever Swamp. Something that howls at night. Something that kills small animals. Everyone thinks it's Grady's dog, Wolf. But Wolf is a nice dog, Grady thinks. Until he spies Wolf howling at the moon—and mysteriously disappearing at midnight!

THE STORY BEHIND THE STORY

Sometimes a single picture will inspire a *Goosebumps* book. Once when R.L. Stine was visiting Florida, he took a short boat ride through a swampy area. He was amazed to see a deer standing right in the middle of the swampy water. That deer stayed in his head—until it appeared in the pages of *The Werewolf of Fever Swamp*!

FRIGHTENING FACTS

How did the werewolf of Fever Swamp become a werewolf? According to ancient legends, there are several ways to become a werewolf. If you are bitten by a werewolf, you're doomed to become one. If you eat meat killed by a wolf, you will turn into a wolfman. If you drink water from a wolf's footprint, you'll change into a werewolf.

Some werewolves become werewolves on purpose. They rub themselves with ointments made from ingredients such as bat's blood, or foxglove, wolfbane and other strange plants. The werewolf of Fever Swamp accidentally started his life as a werewolf with ointments. He was just experimenting—unfortunately, the results were very hairy.

HAVE A GOOD SHRIEK!

Everyone knows this werewolf joke—that's why we've hidden the punchline. Cross out the letters in the word SWAMP. Then unscramble the letters that are left, and you'll find the answer to the joke.

What do you call someone who puts his right arm down a werewolf's throat?

A S Y W A M F P E A A W L P P T

Answer on page 54.

HAND ME A SCARE
from
PIANO LESSONS CAN BE MURDER

GOOSEBUMPS 12

Published October 1994

THE STORY

When Jerry moves into his new house, he can't believe what he finds. Up in the dusty attic, hidden under an old quilt, is a shiny, black piano. As soon as he sees it, Jerry dreams about learning to play. But his dream quickly turns into a nightmare when he meets his new piano teacher—Dr Shreek!

THE STORY BEHIND THE STORY

Enquiring *Goosebumps* fans want to know who the ghost is who plays the piano in Jerry's house. We don't know much, but we do know she was one of Dr Shreek's unfortunate students. Her name was Mara Klane. And she lived in Jerry's house with her dog Dino, a miniature greyhound.

Mara decided to take piano lessons because she was lonely and bored. Too bad for her—she was one of Dr Shreek's most talented students. She had such beautiful hands...

TOTALLY AWESOME! The parts of the book you'll never forget

Goosebumps fans may never forget the creepy Dr Shreek chanting over and over again: "Remember the hands. They're alive. Let them breathe." Ewwwww!

FRIGHTENING FACT

There's only one song mentioned by name in the entire book. It's a song Jerry's mum can play on the piano. To find out what it is, unscramble the letters below.

S I K H P T C O S C

Answer on page 54.

THE LORD HIGH EXECUTIONER
from
A NIGHT IN TERROR TOWER
GOOSEBUMPS 25
Published February 1996

THE STORY

Sue and her brother Eddie are having a great time visiting London. Then they lose their tour group and find themselves locked inside a terrifying prison tower. That's bad. What's worse? They're being followed by an evil stranger cloaked in black ... who wants them dead!

THE STORY BEHIND THE STORY

The Terror Tower is a lot like the Tower of London. That's because the idea for *A Night in Terror Tower* came to R.L. Stine when he was visiting the Tower of London during a trip to England. "I remember I walked up a very narrow staircase," R.L. said. "The stairs twisted round and round, and when I reached the top, I faced a solid wall. It was really creepy. That's what gave me the idea for Terror Tower."

TOTALLY AWESOME! The parts of the book you'll never forget

Goosebumps fans will never forget the most moving words in the book—the words that make Sue and Eddie go back in time. To find the words, go round the circle clockwise, starting with the first letter and writing down every fourth letter.

_ _ _ _ _ _ _, _ _ _ _ _ _ _, _ _ _ _ _ _ _.

Answer on page 54.

START
HERE

↓

S O A U M V R M
R   O
V   A
M   I
U   L
A   V
O S R V M U A O S R

WELCOME TO THE SCARIEST RIDES
from
ONE DAY AT HORRORLAND

GOOSEBUMPS 16

Published March 1995

THE STORY

The Morris family is hopelessly lost. They're searching for Zoo Gardens Theme Park. But they're not having much luck. Then they stumble upon another amusement park. It's called HorrorLand, and it looks kind of cool. Until the Horrors show up—the creepy creatures who work at the park. And those rides. There's something deadly about those rides. Really deadly!

THE STORY BEHIND THE STORY

HorrorLand is run by strange monsters called Horrors. No one knows too much about them. Their story isn't told in *One Day at HorrorLand*.

But they do have a history. The legend goes that fifty years ago, the Horrors were normal people who worked at an old-time funfair. One terribly hot summer, the funfair visited a town in Ohio. And a horrible fire broke out.

The blaze spread quickly. There was no way anyone could have escaped or survived. But when the police searched the smouldering ashes, they discovered—nothing! Not a single trace of the funfair workers.

Rumour has it that those same funfair workers found their way to other employment ... at HorrorLand.

TOTALLY AWESOME! The parts of the book you'll never forget

True *Goosebumps* fans will never forget the ghastliest ride at HorrorLand: The Coffin Cruise—a relaxing Float to the Grave. Lizzy Morris lies down in a real coffin and begins to float downstream. A nice, relaxing ride, until ... the coffin lid slams shut! Lizzy can't open the lid, no matter how hard she pushes. And the air inside the closed dark coffin grows hot. Hot and stale. It's hard to breathe...

Are you a true *Goosebumps* fan? What happens next?

HAVE A GOOD SHRIEK!

What can you order at the HorrorLand Hotel?
Unscramble the letters to find out.

OMOD ERSIVEC

Answer on page 54.

CUDDLES—HE'S ONE HUNGRY HAMSTER!
from
MONSTER BLOOD II

GOOSEBUMPS 18

Published May 1995

THE STORY

No one believes Evan's stories about Monster Blood. Then Evan and his friend Andy feed the green, quivering slime to Cuddles the class hamster. And Cuddles starts growing ... and growing ... and growing...!

THE STORY BEHIND THE STORY

Every kid who's read *Monster Blood II* wants to know more about Conan Barber. He's the bully in Evan's class who's better known as Conan the Barbarian. Conan acts tough, but he has a secret that can now be shared with true *Goosebumps* fans. Conan sleeps with a teddy bear he calls Fluffster, and Conan's mumsie tucks him in every night with a glass of cocoa and a bedtime story. All together now, one, two, three … aaaaah!

HAVE A GOOD SHRIEK!

What time is it when a Monster Blood-eating hamster sits on your bed?
Unscramble the words to find out!

NEW GET A TIME BED TO!

Answer on page 54.

THE PHANTOM STRIKES!
from
PHANTOM OF THE AUDITORIUM

GOOSEBUMPS 29

To be published June 1996

THE STORY

Brooke and her best friend Zeke have won the lead roles in the school play, *The Phantom*. But someone is trying really hard to make sure the play never goes on! Could that someone be ... the Phantom?

THE STORY BEHIND THE STORY

At the end of *Phantom of the Auditorium*, we find out who the Phantom really is. But there are still a lot of questions left unanswered:

● What happened to him 72 years ago that turned him into a phantom?
● Who wrote the play about the Phantom?
● Has the Phantom been haunting Woods Mill Middle School all these years?

Not even R.L. Stine knows the answer to the first two questions. They remain a mystery—for now. But it is definitely true that Woods Mill Middle School is haunted. Just ask any kid who has eaten in the canteen!

TOP SECRET! FOR *GOOSEBUMPS* FANS ONLY!

There's something only Brooke knows about Zeke. Now you can find out, too! Crack the numbers code below to discover the shocking truth...

		S								A	S
19	22	8	7	18	15	15		4	22	26	9	8

								A		A	S
16	22	9	14	18	7		11	2	17	26	14	26	8

Answer on page 54.

SLAPPY—HE WALKS, HE STALKS!
from
NIGHT OF THE LIVING DUMMY

GOOSEBUMPS 7

Published May 1994

THE STORY

What a terrific find! Lindy Powell has uncovered a ventriloquist's dummy. She calls him Slappy and has a great time learning to make him talk. Then Lindy's sister, Kris, gets a dummy of her own. Mr Wood. And that's when the fun stops—and the evil begins. Are the dummies behind it all? No way. Right? Hmmm...

THE STORY BEHIND THE STORY

Slappy is very proud of his family tree, but no one knows the real story of his creation. He claims he's related to the great redwoods, but that sounds like a really tall tale!

Here's what we do know. Slappy looks an awful lot like a dummy R.L. Stine had when he was a kid. R.L. used to try to scare his brother with his dummy. Do you think the two dummies are related? It's possible.

TOTALLY AWESOME! The parts of the book you'll never forget

The magic words that bring Mr Wood to life:
Karru marri odonna loma molonu karrano.
Mr Wood's best lines:
- Is that a moustache, or are you eating a rat?
- Your face reminds me of a wart I had removed!
- If we count your chins, will it tell us your age?

TOP SECRET! FOR *GOOSEBUMPS* FANS ONLY!

Wonder what happened to Slappy after *Night of the Living Dummy*? For really hot news, cross out every Z, A and P below!

CZPOAMPAIZNG ASPOZOZN: ANPIAG-PHZT OPFA ZTPAZHZE AALPZIZVAIZA-APPNG DZUMPMZY IAAIA.

Answer on page 55.

PETRIFYING PUZZLES
AND GRUESOME GAMES

So you think you're a *Goosebumps* fan? Maybe even the ULTIMATE *Goosebumps* fan? Well, here's your chance to show your stuff. These puzzles aren't for kids who've read one or two *Goosebumps* books. They're for the true collector—the kid who likes being scared, all the time, by the creepy creatures that haunt *Goosebumps*.

You can check your puzzle answers on pages 55–56—if you dare!

Let the games begin!

GOOSEBUMPS CAP SLAPPIN' GAME!

Warning: this game is for serious *Goosebumps* fans only.

Okay, you've been warned. If you still want to try your luck, here are the rules. You'll need two or more players for each game. (Not fair using ghosts—you have to be able to see your opponent!) Decide before you start if you're playing for keeps or not.

1   Each player places an equal number of scaredy-caps face up in a single stack.

2   Flip the slammer. Whoever gets the slammer to

land with Curly the skeleton face-up goes first. If you need to, flip three times each and see who gets Curly most often.

3 The first player asks the second player a *Goosebumps* trivia question. Use the questions below, or try one of your own. If the first player answers correctly, he or she gets to throw the Curly slammer down on the stack. He or she keeps any caps that flip over.

4 Restack the remaining caps. Now it's the second player's turn to ask the questions. Keep playing until every scaredy-cap in the pile has flipped over.

5 The player who flips over the most caps wins the game.

Questions:

1 Who is the director at Camp Nightmoon in *Welcome to Camp Nightmare*?
2 How many gold stars does it take to win a prize at the library in Timberland Falls in *The Girl Who Cried Monster*?
3 What is the name of Evan's great-aunt in *Monster Blood*?
4 What does Max find in his attic in *Let's Get Invisible*?
5 While Hannah stays at home in *The Ghost Next Door*, where is her best friend, Janey?

6   What cereal is Skipper Matthews' favourite late-night snack in *Attack of the Mutant*?

7   What kind of bird does Todd Barstow's sister Regina make out of papier mâché in *Go Eat Worms*?

8   Dr Deep has only one rule for Billy and Sheena in *Deep Trouble*—stay away from what?

HIDE AND GO SCARE!

TOP SECRET! FOR *GOOSEBUMPS* FANS ONLY!

When it comes to *Goosebumps*, you never know what (or who) is hiding just around the bend. Hidden in this wordsearch are words from the titles of lots of *Goosebumps* books. First fill in the blanks. Next find the missing words in the wordsearch. Then, to learn the title of the March 1996 *Goosebumps*, unscramble the letters you didn't circle in the wordsearch.

Oh, one last rule. You can't look at your books to find the missing words. Real *Goosebumps* fans don't need to!

1 _____ Cheese and Die!
2 The _____ Next Door
3 Stay Out of the _____
4 Night of the Living _____
5 The _____ of Fever Swamp
6 _____ Lessons Can Be Murder
7 Why I'm Afraid of _____
8 Let's _____ Invisible!
9 Welcome to _____ Nightmare
10 The Haunted _____
11 Be Careful What You _____ For

12 The Scarecrow _____ at Midnight
13 The Girl Who Cried _____
14 The Curse of the Mummy's _____
15 _____ to Dead House
16 You Can't _____ Me!

```
Y  M  O  N  S  T  E  R  M  F
A  W  A  L  K  S  C  K  A  L
S  P  T  S  O  K  M  C  S  O
Y  I  S  C  E  F  A  T  K  W
M  A  O  A  C  M  O  S  I  E
M  N  H  R  P  M  E  S  O  R
U  O  G  E  B  E  H  L  O  E
D  H  O  U  B  O  C  C  O  W
W  E  L  C  O  M  E  G  E  T
T  D  T  N  E  M  E  S  A  B
```

TITLE: _ _ _ _ _ _ _ _ _ _ _ _ _ _ _ _ _ _ _ _

Answer on page 55.

THE WORD IS SCARED

What's your favourite *Goosebumps* story? How about one you and your friends write yourselves?

Gather a bunch of *Goosebumps* fans in one room. Fill in all the blanks by asking for the kind of word written in brackets after the spaces. DO NOT read the story first! When you've finished filling in the blanks, read your terrifying tale out loud.

IT GREW IN THE _____!

(name of room in your house)

I remember when I first saw

_____ . *(something in your refrigerator)*

It was a dark and _____ *(kind of weather)* _____ (part of the day)*.

My brothers and sisters were already

48

tucked into their _____ *(thing in your room)*. But not me. That's the time I picked to go exploring in my parents' _____ *(room in your house)*. All I was looking for was a quick _____ *(something you eat)*. But when I opened the door, my eyes met with a horrible _____ *(thing)*. It was _____ *(size)* and _____ *(colour)* and had _____ *(number)* _____s *(body part)*. I had never seen anything so _____ *(description)*. I ran out of the front door to my neighbour's _____ *(thing)*. The scary thing followed me. And then it turned _____ *(colour)*! So I kept on _____ing *(action word)*. It wouldn't stop chasing me. And the faster it ran, the

_____er *(description)* it got! Aah!

Look out! Here it comes now!

BEWARE OF DOGS (AND CATS)!

Here's a game with some real bite! Match the pet to the *Goosebumps* book it appears in.

1   Whitey
2   Petey
3   Rusty
4   Punkin
5   Barky
6   Trigger

A   Night of the Living Dummy
B   Be Careful What You Wish For
C   The Ghost Next Door
D   Monster Blood
E   Welcome to Dead House
F   Let's Get Invisible!

Answers on page 56.

CREEPY, CRAWLY CROSSWORD

What's a three-letter word for a *Goosebumps* expert?
Y–O–U!

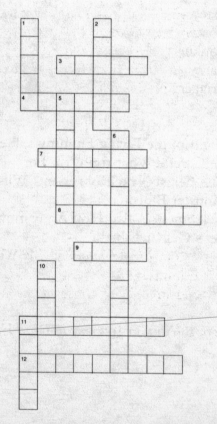

ACROSS

3. Dr Brewer is in danger of becoming a house
_____. (5)

4. Name of the dummy found in the bin in *Night of the Living Dummy*. (6)

7. In *Be Careful What You Wish For*, Samantha plays
_____ball. (6)

8. Gary Lutz's bee-loving next-door neighbour is called Mr _____. (8)

9. What does Grady name the stray dog he finds in *The Werewolf of Fever Swamp*? (4)

11. The signs at HorrorLand: No _____. (8)

12. What hairy creature does Eddie try to drop on Courtney's head in *You Can't Scare Me*? (9)

DOWN

1. What creepy, crawly creatures does Todd Barstow find in his spaghetti? (5)

2. Skipper collects comics. His friend, Wilson, collects rubber _____. (6)

5. In *Monster Blood II*, Evan and Andy move to this city. (7)

6. In *Night of the Living Dummy*, Mr Wood is a
_____'s dummy. (13)

10. Gabe's cousin in *The Curse of the Mummy's Tomb*. (4)

11. Name of the dog in *Welcome to Dead House*. (5)

Answers on page 56.

ANSWERS

COMING SOON: NIGHT OF
THE LIVING DUMMY II

Page 44/45
1. Big Al; 2. six; 3. Kathryn; 4. a magic mirror;
5. at camp; 6. Frosted Flakes; 7. a robin; 8. coral
reefs

Page 46/47
1. Say; 2, Ghost; 3. Basement; 4. Dummy;
5. Werewolf; 6. Piano; 7. Bees; 8. Get; 9. Camp;
10. Mask; 11. Wish; 12. Walks; 13. Monster;
14. Tomb; 15. Welcome; 16. Scare.

```
Y M O N S T E R M F
A W A L K S C K A L
S P T S O K M C S O
Y I S C E F A T K W
M A O C M O S I E
M N H R P M E S O R
U O G E B E H L O E
D H O U B O C C O W
W E L C O M E G E T
T D T N E M E S A B
```

THE CUCKOO CLOCK OF DOOM

Page 51   1F; 2E; 3C; 4B; 5A; 6D

Page 52/3

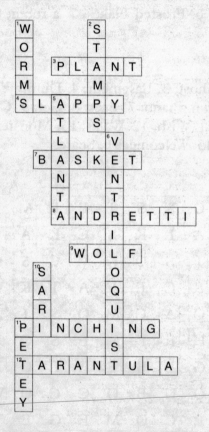

Goosebumps

by R.L. Stine

Reader beware, you're in for a scare!

These terrifying tales will send shivers up your spine . . .

Available now:

Look out for:

The Outfit

Robert Swindells

"Faithful, fearless, full of fun,
Winter, summer, rain or sun,
One for five, and five for one –
THE OUTFIT!"

*Meet The Outfit – Jillo, Titch, Mickey and Shaz. Share in
their adventures as they fearlessly investigate any mystery,
and injustice, that comes their way . . .*

Move over, Famous Five, The Outfit are here!

The Secret of Weeping Wood

The Outfit are determined to discover the truth about the
eerie crying, coming from scary Weeping Wood. Is the
wood really haunted?

We Didn't Mean To, Honest!

The marriage of creepy Kenneth Kilchaffinch to snooty
Prunella could mean that Froglet Pond, and all its
wildlife, will be destroyed. So it's up to The Outfit to
make sure the marriage is off . . . But how?

Kidnap at Denton Farm

Farmer Denton's new wind turbine causes a protest
meeting in Lenton, and The Outfit find themselves in
the thick of it. But a *kidnap* is something they didn't
bargain for . . .

The Ghosts of Givenham Keep

What is going on at spooky Givenham Keep? It can't be
haunted, can it? The Outfit are just about to find out . . .

Reader beware –
here's THREE TIMES the scare!

Look out for these two bumper GOOSEBUMPS
editions. With three spine-tingling stories by
R.L. Stine in each book, get ready for three times
the thrill ... three times the scare ... three times the
GOOSEBUMPS!

GOOSEBUMPS COLLECTION 1
Say Cheese and Die
Welcome to Dead House
Stay Out of the Basement

GOOSEBUMPS COLLECTION 2
The Curse of the Mummy's Tomb
Let's Get Invisible!
Night of the Living Dummy

Hippo Fantasy

Lose yourself in a whole new world, a world where anything is possible – from wizards and dragons, to time travel and new civilizations . . . Gripping, thrilling, scary and funny by turns, these Hippo Fantasy titles will hold you captivated to the very last page.